10 Things You Need to Know About

Being Famous

by Jen Jones

Capstone
press

Mankato, Minnesota

Snap Books are published by Capstone Press,
151 Good Counsel Drive, P.O. Box 669, Mankato, Minnesota 56002.
www.capstonepress.com

Library of Congress Cataloging-in-Publication Data
Jones, Jen.
  Being famous / by Jen Jones.
  p. cm.—(Snap books. 10 things you need to know about)
  Summary: "Explores the highs and lows of being a celebrity, including award shows, dealing with the
paparazzi, and tabloids"—Provided by publisher.
  Includes bibliographical references and index.
  ISBN-13: 978-1-4296-0126-9 (hardcover)
  ISBN-10: 1-4296-0126-4 (hardcover)
  1. Fame. 2. Fame—Social aspects. 3. Awards. 4. Mass media and publicity. 5. Performing arts—Public
relations. I. Title. II. Series.
BJ1470.5.J66 2008
302.5—dc22   2007001314

Editors: Wendy Dieker and Christine Peterson
Designer: Juliette Peters
Photo Researchers: Charlene Deyle and Jo Miller

Photo Credits:
AP/Wide World Photos/ Ric Francis, 7; BigStockPhoto.com/Jim Lopes, 8–9; BigStockPhotos.com/Yuliya Semakova, 23
(right); Corbis/Frank Trapper, 21; Corbis/Patrick Giardino, 4–5; Corbis/Reuters/Fred Prouser, 13; Corbis/Reuters/Mario
Anzuoni, 11 (left); Corbis/Reuters/Mike Blake, 23 (left); iStockphoto/Maciej Laska, cover; Michele Torma Lee, 32; Rex
USA/Charles Sykes, 19; Rex USA/MB Pictures, 17 (right); Shutterstock/ Brian McEntire, 10; Shutterstock/Candice
M. Cunningham, 17 (left); Shutterstock/David Davis, 24–25; Shutterstock/Harvey Fitzhugh, 15; Shutterstock/Ingvald
Kaldhussater, back cover; Shutterstock/Ivan Cholakov, 16; Shutterstock/Kaleena Kruse, 18; Shutterstock/Michal Gach,
6; Shutterstock/Romanchuck Dimitry, 8, 30; Shutterstock/Slavoljub Pantelic, 22; Shutterstock/Stephen Strathdee, 26;
Shutterstock/Steve Broer, 27; ZUMA Press/ Laura Farr, 11 (right)

1 2 3 4 5 6 12 11 10 09 08 07

Table of Contents

Introduction 4

1 Celebrities snag all kinds of free stuff 6

2 Stars say "Cheese" for the paparazzi 8

3 When you're famous, you dress to impress...........10

4 Famous folks love to explore different careers..... 12

5 Tabloids keep celebs on the front page 14

6 In a major city, you're likely to spot some stars.... 16

7 Most celebs have a large posse 18

8 Stars experience different levels of fame........... 20

9 Awards shows are like the proms of stardom 22

10 Celebrities keep connected with their fans.......... 24

A Few More Things You Need to Know........................26

QUIZ: What's Your Hollywood Destiny?.....................28

Glossary... 30

Read More 31

Internet Sites 31

About the Author 32

Index... 32

Introduction

Hollywood is a weird and wonderful place. Stars can become famous for red carpet fashions, dating their co-stars, or simply being fabulously rich. Of course, many celebrities earn their fame by being talented actors, musicians, or models. Whichever way they rise to fame, it's quite a ride once celebs get there.

In this book, you'll learn about the highs and lows of stardom, as well as the celebs' secrets to success. Get ready for the inside scoop on what it's like to be famous.

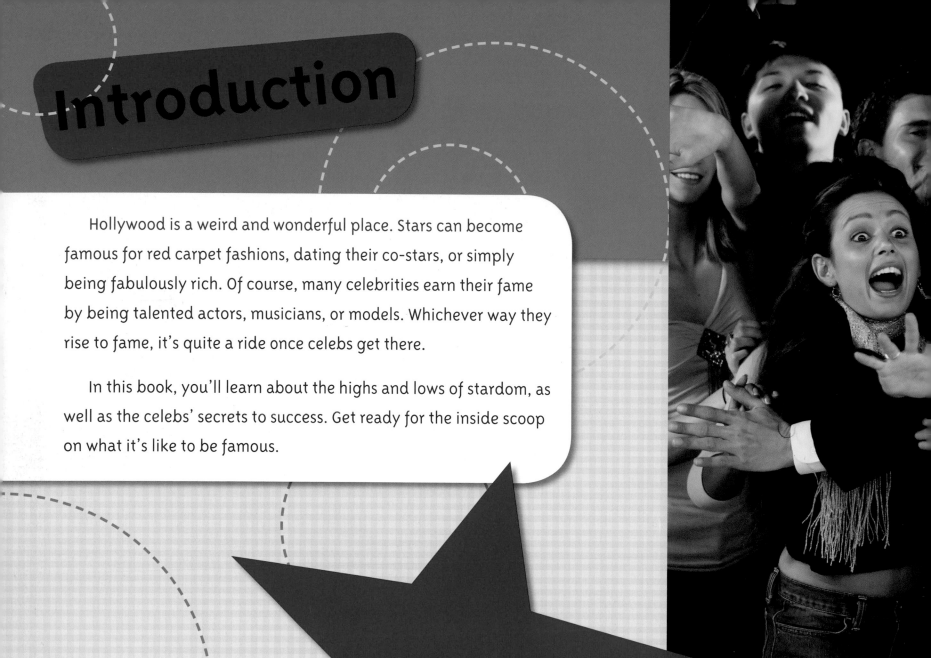

Celebrities snag all kinds of free stuff

Famous people seem to have all the luck. Not only do they have stylish looks and bulging wallets, but they also get loads of free stuff called swag. From designer jeans to crystal-covered Sidekicks, stars receive all kinds of gifts. And forget about paying for dinner at restaurants and clubs. For many places, it's an honor just to have celebs walk through the doors.

At awards shows, celebs get the VIP treatment in gifting rooms. In these exclusive rooms, celebrities get free stuff just for posing with products. Companies get pictures of stars using their stuff, and celebs walk away with new clothes and electronics. It's a win-win situation.

2 Stars say "Cheese" for the paparazzi

Look! Up in the tree! It's a bird, it's a—paparazzi? Yep, these clever celebrity photographers will do anything to get the perfect picture. The biggest stars find it's impossible to leave the house without being caught on film. Photographers wait for them outside restaurants. They lurk on sidewalks and hide in bushes. The paparazzi make it their job to be in the right place at the right time. Why? Magazines and tabloids pay big bucks for hot star shots. Weeklies will pay more than $500,000 for some pictures of celebrity babies or couples!

3 When you're famous, you dress to impress

Stars have lots of money to spend. What better way to spend your cash than on pricey jewelry or designer clothes? Reporters often ask whom celebs are "wearing," so it's important for stars to know the most popular designers. Some top designers include Roberto Cavalli, Giorgio Armani, and Christian Dior.

Whether they're out shopping or strolling the red carpet, stars step out in style. They need to look their best wherever they go. No star wants to hear someone say: "She looks better on screen!" When it comes to style, most stars don't go it alone. They often hire wardrobe stylists to pick the perfect outfits.

Moment of Truth

Since 1960, fashion critic Mr. Blackwell has released a list of the top 10 worst-dressed stars for the year. Britney Spears, Paris Hilton, and Mariah Carey have all been charged with fashion offenses by this style enforcer.

Mr. Blackwell

4 Famous folks love to explore different careers

When a star is on top, the business opportunities pour in. Many stars extend their talents to other careers. They count on their fans to help these new businesses succeed. Look at Hilary Duff. Already popular for her role on *Lizzie McGuire*, she had huge hits as a singer and success with her clothing line, Stuff. This makes her a multi-hyphenate, or a person with more than one main job.

Then there's the ultimate multi-hyphenate: Jennifer Lopez, known as J. Lo to her fans. Follow J. Lo on her fame journey:

- ❀ Highest-paid Latina actress in history
- ❀ Pop star with several best-selling albums
- ❀ Fashion and perfume designer
- ❀ Owner of Madre's Restaurant in Pasadena, California

Now that's what we call multi-talented!

5 Tabloids keep celebs on the front page

Ever seen wild headlines like "Jessica Gets a Nose Job!" or "Is Paris Broke?" Odds are you were looking at a tabloid magazine. These weekly mags print only the newest and nastiest celeb gossip. Tabloids sometimes print stories that stars claim are untrue. Tabloid reporters often use interviews with shady sources who claim they're friends of stars. They print stories based on rumors. Stars have won court cases against tabloids for false stories.

Yet stars also know that these magazines can help their careers. News stories help stars stay in the public eye. Having fans who care about your newest fashion or latest date means that your career is red-hot.

6 In a major city, you're likely to spot some stars

Hollywood stars often seem larger than life. Yet stars still have to go about their daily lives. Travel to major U.S. cities, and you may spot stars shopping for groceries, taking out the trash, or walking their dogs.

Of all the major U.S. cities, Los Angeles may have the most stars per square inch. After all, most film and television work is done there. You can also find celebs in New York City, Chicago, and Miami. Some stars get tired of Hollywood and buy homes in tiny, little-known towns. Julia Roberts has a ranch in Taos, New Mexico. Actress Demi Moore escapes to her home in Hailey, Idaho.

Stargazing

When visiting Los Angeles, there are certain places where you're almost guaranteed to see a star. Take a trip to Robertson Boulevard, where you'll find Kitson and the Ivy. Kitson is a pricey shop with a red-carpet entrance. Paris Hilton and Lindsay Lohan often shop there. The Ivy is a posh restaurant and regular star hangout.

7 Most celebs have a large posse

Just in case you thought celebs stay famous on their own, think again. There's a whole pack of people who help a star each day. Agents and managers find jobs for stars and secure hefty paychecks. Personal assistants do everything from getting dry cleaning to making appointments. And let's not forget the style team. Every star's team includes a wardrobe stylist, makeup artist, and hairstylist. These masters of fashion and beauty are paid big bucks to help stars go glam. Add in a celebrity's bodyguards, friends, family, and other employees, and you've got an entourage. All these people play a role in furthering a star's career.

8 Stars experience different levels of fame

From household name to hall of shame, there are many levels of fame. The most popular stars are on the A-list. This list includes the highest-paid and most recognized stars. A-listers include Julia Roberts and George Clooney.

Next down on the ladder are B-list celebs. These stars are either on the rise or fall. Jessica Alba is an example of a star on the rise. She got her start in teen movies like *Never Been Kissed*. Now she is heading toward A-list status with some starring roles in films like *Sin City* and the *Fantastic Four*.

Last but not least is the D-list. Known as "famous for being famous," these stars are seen as lacking talent. Stars of reality shows and socialites are often lumped in this group.

9 Awards shows are like the proms of stardom

Hollywood often seems like high school, and awards shows are a perfect example. Like teens preparing for prom, stars spend months getting ready for awards shows. They stress over selecting glam gowns, dieting, and finding the perfect date. To win an award, stars must be nominated by others. Sounds like the prom royalty, doesn't it? At the awards show, the stars strut their stuff on the red carpet before crowds of photographers and cheering fans. After the awards are presented, stars dance the night away at huge parties.

Hollywood Cheat Sheet

Not sure what each awards show is all about? Use this handy reference tool:

❀ The Emmy Awards honor the best television shows and stars.

❀ The Grammy Awards recognize the finest singers and music makers of the year.

❀ The Academy Awards, or "Oscars," honor actors and other professionals who create movies.

10 Celebrities keep connected with their fans

In today's digital age, fans can easily connect with their favorite stars. Years ago, fans had to join special clubs to keep tabs on stars. Now they can simply log onto a celeb's MySpace page or personal Web site to get the scoop. Stars like Britney Spears and John Mayer even keep online blogs to share their thoughts with fans.

Thanks to technology, fans also have the power to make stars. Shows like *American Idol* and *Total Request Live* (TRL) allow viewers to call in or text message votes for their favorite singers. Without the American public, stars like Kelly Clarkson and Carrie Underwood would still be unknowns.

Stars have really awesome homes

From private movie theaters to kitchens fit for a king, celebrity homes have it all. Driving the streets of star-filled cities like Beverly Hills, Los Angeles, and Miami is a great way to see these amazing mansions. Can't quite make it that far? Check out a show like *MTV Cribs*, where stars like Usher and Missy Elliott show off their posh estates.

Famous people travel the world

When stars are promoting a new film, CD, or TV show, they often go on worldwide press tours. Stars may even visit several cities in one day to do interviews with local reporters. Though it may seem glamorous to jet around the world, it can also be exhausting.

Celebrities sometimes change their names

Celebrities rarely have super-long names. Stars are often asked to change their names if they're hard to say or "unpleasant" to the ear. For instance, Tom Cruise's real name is Thomas Mapother IV. Some stars just shorten their names to become one-name divas. Madonna's full name is Madonna Louise Ciccone.

Some stars didn't always have glamorous jobs

When still unknown, some future stars took strange jobs to pay the bills. Kelly Clarkson once sold vacuums. Johnny Depp sold pens by phone. Yet Brad Pitt's odd job tops that. He once dressed as a giant chicken for a fast-food chain, standing on a street in 100-degree heat!

What's Your Hollywood Destiny?

You're stuck on a plane for four hours. How do you pass the time?

A Watch your favorite DVD
B Hum along to your iPod
C Strike up a chat with your neighbor

What's your favorite TV show?

A *Inside the Actors' Studio*
B *American Idol*
C *E! News Live*

You can take a trip anywhere in the world. Where do you go?

A New York City—Broadway here you come!
B New Orleans—jazz and jambalaya are your favs!
C Jamaica—you need a break!

Who's your Hollywood idol?

A Movie star Natalie Portman
B Pop singer Christina Aguilera
C TV and radio host Ryan Seacrest

At school, you're known as:

A A drama queen and star of school plays
B A music expert who knows her Timberlake from her T.I.
C The chatty one who's always in trouble for talking in class

What awards show would you most want to attend?

A The Oscars
B The Grammys
C The Emmys

When you throw parties, what's your favorite activity?

A Charades
B Karaoke
C Truth or Dare

What terrifies you the most?
- Ⓐ Losing your cool
- Ⓑ Losing your voice
- Ⓒ Losing your friends

What would you be voted for in the yearbook?
- Ⓐ Most Likely to Succeed
- Ⓑ Best Sense of Humor
- Ⓒ Most Spirited

What would your role be at a football game?
- Ⓐ Holding court as a cheerleader
- Ⓑ Belting out the national anthem
- Ⓒ Announcing from the broadcasting booth

Where do you fit into your family?
- Ⓐ Youngest child
- Ⓑ Middle child
- Ⓒ Oldest child

Which city are you most like?
- Ⓐ Los Angeles
- Ⓑ Nashville
- Ⓒ London

What group do you belong to at school?
- Ⓐ Drama club
- Ⓑ Choir
- Ⓒ Debate team

What's your favorite show to watch on the Disney Channel?
- Ⓐ *High School Musical*
- Ⓑ *Hannah Montana*
- Ⓒ *That's So Raven*

Who would your Hollywood BFF be?
- Ⓐ Beverley Mitchell, TV's *7th Heaven* star
- Ⓑ Jessica Simpson, pop singer and movie star
- Ⓒ Vanessa Minnillo, ET correspondent

When scoring your answers, Ⓐ equals 5 points, Ⓑ equals 3 points, and Ⓒ equals 1 point. Total them up and find out your Hollywood destiny!

1-25 = You're naturally talkative and at ease with others. Watch out, TRL hosts — here comes the new on-screen queen!

26-50 = Whether belting out pump-me-up dance songs or show tunes, you've got the right stuff to be a singer. Someone hand this girl a mic!

51-75 = When the curtain calls, you're front and center. Being an actress is a dream come true for you!

Glossary

entourage (ahn-too-RAHZH)—a group of people who follow and attend to celebrities

multi-hyphenate (muhl-tee-HYE-fuhn-ate)—a person who has many different careers at the same time

nominate (NOM-uh-nate)—to suggest that someone would be the right person for an award or honor

paparazzi (pah-puh-RAHT-see)—aggressive photographers who take pictures of celebrities for sale to magazines or newspapers

socialite (soh-SHUH-lahyt)—a person who is popular in society

tabloid (TAB-loid)—a newspaper that contains brief stories and pictures that are meant to stir up interest or cause excitement

Read More

Israel, Elaine. *Hilary Duff.* Today's Superstars. Milwaukee: Gareth Stevens, 2007.

Parish, James Robert. *Jennifer Lopez: Actor and Singer.* Ferguson Career Biographies. New York: Ferguson, 2006.

Wessling, Katherine. *Backstage at a Movie Set.* Backstage Pass. New York: Children's Press, 2003.

Internet Sites

FactHound offers a safe, fun way to find Internet sites related to this book. All of the sites on FactHound have been researched by our staff.

Here's how:
1. Visit *www.facthound.com*
2. Choose your grade level.
3. Type in this book ID **1429601264** for age-appropriate sites. You may also browse subjects by clicking on letters, or by clicking on pictures and words.
4. Click on the **Fetch It** button.

FactHound will fetch the best sites for you!

About the Author

The first time Jen Jones saw the Hollywood sign, she almost fainted! When she's not reading up on pop culture or celebs, she makes her living as a freelance writer in Los Angeles. Her stories have been published in magazines such as *American Cheerleader*, *Dance Spirit*, *Ohio Today*, and *Pilates Style*. She has also written for E! Online and PBS Kids, and has been a Web site producer for major talk shows such as *The Jenny Jones Show*, *The Sharon Osbourne Show*, and *The Larry Elder Show*. She has also written books on gymnastics and fashion for young girls.

Index

awards shows, 6, 22, 23

Blackwell, Mr., 11
blogs, 24
businesses, 12

Duff, Hilary, 12

entourages, 18

fame levels, 20
fashion, 4, 6, 10, 11, 12, 14, 18, 22

Hollywood, 4, 16, 22
homes, 16, 26

Ivy, The, 17

Kitson, 17

Lopez, Jennifer, 12
Los Angeles, 16, 17, 26

names, 27

paparazzi, 8

red carpet, 4, 10, 17, 22
reporters, 10, 14, 26

stylists, 10, 18
swag, 6

tabloids, 8, 14
travel, 16, 26